Tonight Not
Even My Skin

*I found some previous lives in a cardboard
box, and thought I'd give them air...*

Tonight Not Even My Skin

Selected Poems by
Leanne Ponder

Eastern Coyote Press

Esquire Magazine
"The Poet" Sept. 1976
"Rumplestiltskin" Aug. 1976
"The Furniture Mover" Nov. 1977

Literature East and West
"Sincerity Paper" March 1974

South Dakota Review
"Poem Written While Waiting for a Plane" &
"His Fair Lady" Winter 1971/1972

Four Quarters
"Earth Counts Time" "Nomad" & "Fat Girl" 1975

Northwest Review
"Pinball Machine" 1970

Poet & Critic
"Looking Up From Paradise" 1971

Truck
"Lonely With My Dog" 1973

Mississippi Review
"Suburbia, or This House is a Whale of a Buy, Mrs.
Jones" 1973

for Tim

Contents

The Poet..3

•§•

Pinball Machine.......................................7
His Fair Lady..8
Ode To A Blacksnake...............................9
Sincerity Paper.......................................10
Rumplestiltskin.......................................12
Tonight Not Even My Skin.......................14

•§•

Even Remembered Your Mouth.................17
Looking Up From Paradise.......................18
Adam Gave Each Animal a Name.............20
Lonely With My Dog................................21
2 Rejection Slips & Divorce Papers............22
Poem Written On I89N............................23

•§•

Fat Girl..27
Snapshots...28
Nomad...29
Suburbia..30
The Collusion...31
Parting...32

•§•

Lullaby...34
Christening In Darkness 36
She Says..37
The Furniture Mover 38
Prayer 39
Earth Counts Time..................................40

•§•

He Who Rides Out From The Sun 43
I Am Weaving A Portrait 44
Once We Wore Red Ochre 46
Shadows, Ashes, Desert Prayers 48

•§•

Ceremony 53
Margins...57
The Lady and The Sun..............................56
Waiting for a Plane 59

•§•

Invitation to a Country Gentleman 67

•§•

Leanne Ponder..71

The Poet

"A page is no place for a poem," he said,
laying down his pen
to write a sonnet with his tongue
on her
astonished
skin.

The Pinball Machine

It was strange, her being such a lady and all,
but he was her game,
and she had a knack for playing.
She could flip out accusations
like her tongue had a spring to it,
ricocheting them from one guilt to another,
buzzing each like dentists' drills on nerves.
And he, not knowing he was being played,
would light up with apologies
give free games,
and never tilt.

His Fair Lady

Before we met, my bones were disarrayed:
tablelegs shuddered when I passed,
merchants never let their prayer beads rest.
I clattered against myself.
My bones, like pickup sticks tossed in the air,
formed sporadic stars,
then landed in absurd heaps
of unrelated parts.

I lived in a kaleidoscope,
stumbled through the dancing pieces,
shattered life to fragile patterns,
never asking reasons.
(But every stumble brought new shimmering prisms.)

Then you set upon me like a paint-by-numbers man
confronted by a Jackson Pollack canvas.
Was it my clumsiness inspired you
to outline all my edges?
To lay my bones in tidy rows?
To collate my bright colors?

Now I sit, my bones composed,
ankles crossed like Roman numerals,
captured by your loving.
Darling, are you listening?
Aren't you ever frightened by the sound
of nothing breaking?

Ode to a Blacksnake

Blacksnake,
muscling through my fingers
like a thick and endless wrist,
I imagined you'd be slimy
as a licked-on licorice stick;
but you glide immaculate across my skin,
dapper in patent leather scales,
wrap me in prehensile bracelets,
flick your grey twig tongue
to taste the odor of my neck,
my cheek; stare in patient
and unlidded calm
while I stroke your nose with my finger.

I must forget I saw you
strike the small mouse unaware,
unhinging your jaws in greed,
taking her on eye to eye,
sucking down her tail
like a strand of pink spaghetti.

Chisso Corporation's President, Kenichi Shimada, signed a "sincerity paper," expressing official regret that the people of the small fishing village of Minamata were being blinded, crippled and killed by mercury-laden shellfish, a result of the industrial wastes Chisso Corporation had been pouring into Minamata Bay since 1968. Mr. Shimada stated the paper was not an admission of legal responsibility.

Sincerity Paper: A Mother's Comment

President Shimada
has signed a public paper
regretting that my daughter
dropped rotting from
the waters of my womb.
An abalone captured
in the mad eye of the sun,
her heart's been bound for eighteen years
in a body blind as bone.
Blind to all sensation,
to the task of asking questions,
each day she lies more rigid
in my arms. She does not know
I stroke her hands,
those useless knobs gnarled inward,
wrenched toward the constant pain
of trying not to die.

Sometimes I think I'll take a stone
and splinter her mute shell.
Inside, I know, she must be beautiful.

Rumplestiltskin

I could have asked for more:
to lie between her thighs,
white birch in Spring;
sing, a thrush, between them,
my body's dreams when young,
and even then ugly as a roach
scuttling between the jeers of children.

"Humpback!" They'd dance the curse around me,
poke my shoulder's stone
with such pretty little fingers.
Pretty like she is: she
whose maiden blood I gave the king.
I gave it, yes, for she
had vowed me anything
to spin the straw to gold.

I should have had her then,
wrapped her like a bib beneath my chin,
wound her like gold thread around my spindle.
But no, I spun for trinkets:
a silver chain, a ring.
She didn't even thank me.

How small the homely dream,
being used to nothing.
She bargained for her life, a kingdom;
I merely for one child
from a womb fecund as Spring.

What we know we learn again.
I swear I'll dream no more.
Love trails beauty like a one man dog
and snarls the rest
like beggars from its door.

Tonight not even my skin

Tonight not even my skin
can hold me close enough
to dispel this solitude
I've chosen. There is something close
to danger when the wind fills
all hollows and the moon
calls from my bed with radiant
tongue. I've been told there are dreams
so intimate one doesn't
dare wake to know them. All night
I've sat like this,
one hand clutching the other
like a talisman.

Even Remembered   Your Mouth

Even remembered   your mouth
Slow & clever
connoisseur
takes over my skin
& speaks of dying
not stopping until
I not with words
understand
that perfect hunger
of wine saying Yes
as it rolls to darkness
over the tongue.

Looking Up From Paradise
(Notes From Jamaica)

Here fruit brawls in trees:
green and orange coconuts
squeeze for place in each palm's crotch
like thirteen piglets at eight teats,
and ackees bunched on fragile stems
finally burst their scarlet skins
to drop three seeds that look like beetles
floating down on swollen wings.

If this is paradise,
where is there space to dream?
Everywhere another seed
is taking root or dying
while natives crowd the marketplace,
voluptuous as plums,
softly bruising word on word
as promises merge to bargains.

They tell this story here:
Once a virgin, in a dream,
ate three ackee seeds
and so gave birth to three fine sons,
black with shining wings.

One son braced his mother's head,
the other two her feet,
and flew into a night so black
none saw where they went.

They say that on the darkest nights
they still can hear her sing.
She has escaped. They lift their heads
toward that song, and dream.

Adam Gave Each Animal A Name

Men howl me down like hounds,
musk haunting their lungs.
But for wounds that taught me how to run
they'd wear me dripping from their mouths
unnamed, heart drained hollow.

How they yearn for what they see:
ripe meat clinging to the bone.
They watch me, one of many sheep,
shear me with one sweep of their eyes.
"HEY!" they shout, and "How about it?"
And I see me hanging in their minds
anonymous on thick meat hooks,
belly slashed empty of sighs.

I was bred to feast on:
my sturdy Mormon kin
fed me on whole grain,
kept me in a tiny pen
of thou-shalt-nots.
Well, I've disowned such doctrine
but still recall that Adam
gave each animal a name.

Lonely with My Dog

Lonely with my dog
I've taken on her ways:
express myself in whines and groans,
cast suspicious eyes at strangers,
run through sprinklers,
disdain forks,
sleep curled against the floor,
shudder in worn nightmares
of undug bones,
lost rabbits,
angry guns.

And when the siren comes dog-whistle shrill,
laser sounds of other accidents,
we join the cry
heads back blind-eyed,
howling
howling.
And with us wolves on mountains,
Trojan women,
all the holy mad.

On Receiving Two Rejection Slips
and Divorce Papers on the Same Day

I got your rejection slip today.
"Without delay this court," it says,
"does order and adjudge
the Plaintiff unable to use (anymore)
the Defendant; therefore the marriage
between them is declared hereby dissolved."

I will not question your editing.
I've revised myself so many times, trying to mind-read your taste,
scotch-taping on new attitudes, erasing myself piece by piece
until my face has become a page of unrelated expressions:
symbolic fiction no one understands;
and my hands wave like parentheses cupping empty air,
unable to hold any explanation together.

My storyline wanders with no transitions,
no simple words to subjugate loneliness to reason.
My heart's composed of consonants (passion lurks in vowels);
And, yes, my name hangs over me
like a poorly-chosen title.

Poem Written on Interstate 89 North

Back on the highway again.
SKI MADONNA EXIT 9
Yes, I'll go there too sometime:
flash my smile like tinfoil,
draw the pretty strangers in,
their faces chattering over me
anonymous as crows
charmed by trivialities
they'd soon enough grow used to.
Women, puppies, will-be,
would-be, have-been, right-now men:
I give them each the best
of what I am — the first edition
autographed goodbye.

A new sky lies at the end of each curve;
I pass by houses I'll never own
where homicide simmers with love in each kitchen;
but my only fighting word is goodbye,
so I'm high on the rumble of wheels
with a week's worth of anecdotes to tell
(none of them true about me).
Tomorrow someone I don't know
will bring words in bouquets,

wind his rhymes around me,
challenge me to stay.
Stay: the word I live on,
but every story needs the tension
of knowing words will end.

The sun rolls to the crest of the mountain;
What time is it now?
Half-past Massachusetts.
Six hours till tomorrow.

Fat Girl

When I was a Fat Girl
in a sausage skin,
tied with ribbons at one end
and shoe strings at the other,
my mother pulled me through stores behind her
like something she'd return
if she could find the manager.

Snapshots

An old story: after twenty years
of French toast and The Times,
sketching sailboats off Bar Harbor,
snapshots of their daughter,
gopher-cheeked, puffing at three candles
or sullen behind dark glasses as sixteen,
her husband left her.

She shows another snapshot to her daughter.
"Weren't we happy then?"
At the beach, arms draped like towels
around each other, the three of them stand
squinting at the sun,
as if it had just asked a question
they cannot answer.

Nomad

I wander like an insatiable nomad
on your skin,
incoherently fragile
heart like a Bedouin's veil
fluttering
until
more than anything
I feel
your eyes; your mouth covers me
like hungry scarlet roses;
your teeth startle my breasts
like quick, incredible snow.
(I know it is not reasonable to love
but I've heard tales of ancient men on endless deserts
who have quenched their thirst
from mirages.)

Suburbia, or
this House is a Whale of a Buy, Mrs. Jones

My house swallowed me.
Its doors are swollen shut
like raw tonsils:
and water clogs like phlegm in drains,
blocking faucets,
every new escape.

This beast is sick: its peristalsis stopped!
Every room is overstocked
with highchairs, ovens, bureaus and divans.
(Such costly excrement.)
Perhaps if I turned every burner on—
broiler, grill and oven too—
a fire would grow to cough me out of here.

But when I run to stare through plate-glass eyes
at strangers, lovers— all outside—
who suck in love as eels suck cray
(Small plankton— love— for endless mouths),
I pull the shades like eyelids into sleep.
If I escaped, how would I then escape?

The Collusion

The Hunter whispered, "I've prayed for you;"
The Deer answered, "I do."
His spear cried her down to her knees;
She felt her bowels burning and called it love.
He bottled her eyes to gaze just at him;
She labeled the bottle Devotion.
He flayed her skin for a shelter;
She called it making a home.
He swallowed her tongue;
She called it passion.
He scrambled her brains for breakfast;
She brewed coffee to wash them down.

"You're guilty too!" he cried.
She whispered, "Your will is my wish."
He sued for divorce on grounds of adultery,
naming as correspondant, Death.

Parting

It isn't that he left, but how:
joking, damp and happy from the shower
he always took to wash off evidence
of semen, sweat and kisses,
to purify himself for one
he claimed he did not love.

I knew of course that someday he (or I)
would leave; but I had pictured anger, tears,
or at least a great relief from the passion
impermanence creates. But he gave no hint
of parting, only kissed my mouth, my cheek,
and licked his lips as if I were a feast
he would return to. Then he said something gay
I can't recall, turned full smile toward me,
started up his car, and drove away
smile, love and all, leaving not a woman
but an audience.

Lullaby

The car veers
as I dream
the sea grows deeper
I fall into

you
stand oval-mouthed
staring from a cliff
as I drift   too
far away
flotsam
into fright

It is not cold I shout
to comfort you
who cannot hear
the water beginning to swallow

Christening in Darkness

The closet named his sins when he was four.
Locked with the dark behind its door, he learned
to be as quiet as a coat. There, closed
in with his mother's shadow swaying huge
and dim from hangers, her shape repeated
again and again like a blind parade
of jurors listening, even his breath
seemed evidence against him. Nothing spoke
in his behalf. Not the small, unfrivolous
hats wrapped smug in white tissue and cake-shaped
boxes; not the long, solemn gloves, pressed flat
as if saying prayers palm to palm in their
plastic sheaths. Wicked, she'd called him. The word
wrapped its dark wrath around him as he knelt
in dread among empty shoes and dying
perfumes. He lifted his lips toward it
as to a mother's cheek. Wicked. It froze
in his throat, and he sang, soft, rocking deep
in the heartbeat of fear. Wicked: a prayer.
Wicked. Wicked. He chanted it over
and over: a litany which finally
became a dream. A lullaby. His name.

She Says,

"For years no one has held me
Except in a functional way. As one
Might hold a bar of soap. I remember
One man sliding my body against
His until the task was done.
How I loved him anyway,
Dreaming of that night until
Another night, another man.
In this manner, my heart, like soap,
Grows smaller."

The Furniture Mover

She looked so sure of love, that stranger:
a piece of hand-rubbed furniture
comfortable in an atmosphere
of oriental rugs, cut-glass
and darkbound books he couldn't name.
He took time off from crating chairs
to kill her. With what other passion could he
move that stranger, hand-rubbed stranger
with her sack of groceries balanced against the door?

Later he tore the sack open to find only
common things; White Rain shampoo,
a wedge of cheese, hamburger and assorted cans.
His dreams had lied again.

And what dim dreams had dragged her to the floor,
forced back her tongue with batting, bound wrists
   with cord too soft to mar the skin?

What prize did he dream her body contained
when he opened it carefully as a carton?

His photograph hit all the morning papers.
Moved furniture for fourteen years and never
broke a thing, he told reporters.

Prayer

Lord, save us from the frightened
who reach only for those
they love so little
losing will not hurt.

Earth Counts Time

Snow has broken the sky,
taken over the trees;
animals curl like parentheses
in burrows. They know this whiteness
is no flag of peace;
it's the crust of milk
on a breast gone hard and mean.

But every meanness has its season,
earth counts time beneath her skin
and I tell myself I'll thrive again
as I lie awake in this cabin,
building up layers of chill,
with your memory slowly circling
like a hawk that has spotted its kill.

He Who Rides Out From The Sun

He who rides out from the sun:
your other dream, the dark one,
knows where your terror lies
and names it love. Your heart
like the hoofbeats beneath him,
thick ribs lifting between his thighs,
guides him blind toward you.
It will not help to write lists
or polish silver. It will not help
to measure the room with your steps.
No order you construct is strong enough.

Even now outside your window
his horse forms white blossoms
with its breath. He has come
and your skin will never again
believe in the logic of its dimensions.
It will slide around him like light,
like an oyster over the tongue.
Tonight all your explanations
will burn, as you look on their ashes
with otherworld eyes, like a child
waving back to relatives whose names
are already forgotten.

I am Weaving a Portrait

(In their rugs, Navajos traditionally weave one strand of grey yarn from center to border. This allows the weaver's spirit to escape after the rug is finished.)

I am weaving a portrait of you.
On the bottom border
condors unleash their wings
like silver prayers in another
language. On days stark with sun
or so dark you can't find your name,
they will fly you to me.

Under each of your feet
a blessing, woven in black
from crushed twigs & leaves of sumac.
These words are yours to keep.
They will walk with you, immense

as friends. My love, from
the beginning I've known
I could weave this portrait until
age curves my hands in, rigid
as branches of piñon. Today
in joy, & perhaps forever,
I am blessed with skill to compose
your heart as a rainbow so vast
with color, my spirit seems lost there

and singing. Yet my hands, trained
in caution, will weave in a thin
grey strand, winding like
a wayward vein to meet
the tapestry's selvage. A safeguard,
not an omen. Still,

in this weaving so vivid in love
I ask you to forgive
this evidence of fear
ordained by custom. This path
which speaks so clearly of grief,
so little of consolation.

Once We Wore Red Ochre

Once we wore red ochre,
bright hue of the dead.
In a common grave
earth pressed our eyelids closed.
Prayers, ancient even then,
filled the air then dimmed
in a pulse of roots
and serenade of worms.
Our hair wove blankets around us;
rain found our hearts and joined them.
Together, moving back in time,
our skins became reptilian:
dried, cracked, said goodbye.
Our long bones gleamed like veins of gypsum.

How long did we share one breath with the ground,
clutching our knees and waiting?
Like Navajos in the first world of fire,
second of air, third of water,
we watched for a signal to dance
toward the sun, trembling
like cicadas dreaming of wings.
How could I not have loved you?

"Myths," Sallustius claimed,
"are things which never happened
but always are." And in what other
way can I explain
this familiar tapestry of our bones,
this song our skins,
as if remembering, sing?

Shadows, Ashes, Desert Prayers

What obstinate blood we shared
as if the web of filament root
woven beneath this New Mexican sand
connected us like veins,
compelling us again and again
to come together in hope
and leave in pain. Those last years
if I loved you at all
it was in that unfair way
some women love alcoholic
men: not for what they are
but could be, if. Oh, Mother,
what you could have been!
But perhaps the ifs go too far back
to know. Before my birth
you'd cursed my brother, your son,
blaming him for your despair,
describing the razor you'd use
to open your wrist, locking
yourself behind bathroom doors,
calculating like a vicious
gardener the silence and time
it would take his screams to grow.

Did I spit up your milk sensing poison?
All creatures hold in their cells a vision
of the inherited predator.

A hawk shadow: new chicks scatter;
but whose wing was I to hide under
when Mother and raptor, shadow
and shelter were one?
Now I search brown photographs,
trying to learn when the shape
of that shadow began. But you look
the same as your friends, another
child in ill-fitting gingham
ludicrous ribbon looped in your hair
as if some giant butterfly
had believed such gold a flower.
Oh, Mother, how much easier
if you'd set the neighbor's Ford on fire
or scrawled lewd pictures in frames
of hopscotch squares. Then I'd have known
for certain to trust the fear of shadows.

I was a child you would not have chosen:
silent, headstrong, and never quite pretty;
then and now like this desert you hated:
compelling for reasons no one could name.
"I used to feel guilty," you told me, "whipping
you so long, so hard, so often.
But you wouldn't cry; you'd grit your teeth
and stare me down, making me
whip you again." I don't remember

the whippings, Mother, only the pain
of watching you touch with such reverence
the porcelain girls gathered on your dresser,
tiny, beautiful and dumb,
shading themselves with parasols
as if the mirror were sun. Yet we tried
to love each other. We tried
as illiterates touch words
in books: blind-fingered, longing
to understand until they burn
in desperation the books which point
so clearly to their failings.

As last night you burned, Mother,
The young man at the crematory
called the bright blue ovens retorts:
replies made in anger. But no reply
is strong enough to dispel wholly
the power of hope gone wrong.
Now on this desert I scatter
your ashes, fragments of teeth
and bone, frightened that multiplied mouths
will open and say I still will not love you.
Oh, Mother, all words are prayers and erratic
shadows of birds who have lost their way home.
And the ashes of your heart
cling to the sage, small greywhite
buds resolute, refusing to blossom.

Ceremony

They are here: animals she's never seen
or dared remember. With luminous eyes
and swaying tails, they offer themselves like flowers
with love. Her husband trails in a different
dream, naming common trees for her instruction.
She does not see the trees he names, only
these beasts who lay her heart open with questions.

Be with me, she calls to her husband, too far
away to hear. The animals circle
as if they'd have her touch them. Suns rise from
their skins. She reaches out to one whose eyes
beg her free from reason, whose tongue curls around
her fingers like butter. Our dreams are the same,
it tells her. Trembling, they exchange skins.
The world, huge, fraught with visions, gathers one breath.

Husband, hold me. This, my dream,
against all reason
will happen.

Margins

He comes home early one day.
curls on his side in bed,
shivering, gathering knees to chest:
a question mark with no answers.
He can't delay or explain the tears.
Something in his eyes is broken.

His wife leans over him, lips moving.
Waiting for her words, he dreams
of searching through an album,
photographs wherein
a woman leans over a photograph
of a dreaming man.
The dream is this: he's trapped by margins,
their white cage slowly closing in
until he crouches in a space
so small not even death can find him.

And certainly not love.
not she whose cool hand solemnly
tests his forehead now for fever,
so young she once persuaded him
surely one more kiss could save,
one more song sung skin to skin.

What is she saying now?
Her soft words break before they reach him.
So young, how can he let he let her know
she has always lived alone,
loved by someone far away.

Far away, he dreams.

The Lady And The Sun

The sun has made her with child;
it could be nothing else.
She has heard its emissaries whisper
soft ghosts rising from skin
telling how close she's been
to answering all questions, No.

In the country of rain she had waited,
filled with her own ashes,
deciphering the mist
on windowpanes (erratic
hieroglyphics; every day
the message changed) until
her husband, vague as each
night's dreams, consulted doctors
who suggested sun.

So she came with her maid
to this isle of stone
pocked with ancient tombs
where goats pulled at their chains
and the hot sweet breath of mimosa
and lemon frightened her. Even
the sea threatened like an unnamed
animal guarding the feet of heaven.

For five days she hid in the cottage,
sending the maid for oranges
fish and wine, as the sun
posed on the horizon, flamboyant
as a magician.   Naked.   Brilliant.
Burning the edge of sea.
On the sixth day he called her name
and she rose, a dreamer
accompanying her body
like a stranger to a cove
where no one watched except the sun.

There she dropped her robe,
brazen and uncertain,
afraid to speak, wrapped
in rays of sun that, like a lover's
fingers, knew her skin.

There by the cyprus   there
and there   by the sea who licked
her pure of fear   the brilliant
hunger of the sun

held her stunned   half-mute
half-flame   until she slid
          ophidian

out of anguish and dead skin
to lie before him new
exhausted   shining

A gecko sprawls on a stone,
swivels its head to watch
her pass;   its eyes, her skin
as gold as sun. Bending
to gather a handful of shells
curved like pastel cradles,
she wonders how she'll explain
the strangeness of the child
who will rise knowing all from her womb,
curl in her arms like a flame.

Poem Written While Waiting for a Plane to Take Me to My Sometimes Husband

Husbamd   a distant word
distant
perhaps as you will be
even when I descend on metal steps
step careful   smiling   towards you

or towards a memory
a childhood home familiar from the street
but inside fire-gutted
or maybe revamped by some chic she
complete with red carpets
and swinging chandeliers

I will be controlled
a stark-black bottle full of fireflies
offer my hand while waiting for your arms

as if they did not matter
as if the words
which tore our love like fragile cloth
were only past

(Jets scream along the runway
  as if it hurts to fly)

How many times I've lied
lied you into monster hood
for men I care for less than you
I recreate myself for strangers
juxtapose a rose against a stone
How frail I am for those who'd have me frail

(The airport halls are like a rich man's tomb
marble with concession stands for mourners)

I am Concourse A
Men have hurried through my halls
horny passengers
candy in one hand   flight bag in the other
Only you stayed
Burned your suitcase in a fit of caring
Fed me flowers   beefsteak   horseshit   time
(I craved everything but candy)
Sank roots into my hungry soil
a farmer with one acre left to plow

God   how I flourished
Grew every crop you sowed
Save one

How lucky, they say now
How lucky you have no children

Beauty-shop brains thriving on cliché
earthworms feeding from the soil
of other people's sorrows
And my heart sinks from them
but I borrow their cliche
 Yes, I say   aren't I lucky
until finally they slide away
smiling
in search of other dying

The plane bounces like a buggy down the runway
and I   strapped safely in
am never safe from loving
never safe
from memories of words and guns and kisses
explosions in continuum
The sign says TAXI WITH CAUTION
but when one engine whirls
echoing the other I am lifted
as I once was in your arms
trembling
toward neither the beginning nor the end.

Girl at a Bus Stop

She has stayed at the magician's too long.
Her heart is a satchel, open
and empty.
Not one bright scarf left.

The Unspoken Word

My shining friend,
how can I say goodbye
when every time I try
my heart feels like a woman
calling come home
to children whose deaths
she wants to believe she dreamed.

Invitation to a Country Gentleman

We will let the horses lead us
along the path of many travelers
who have not known their way to joy
until they found in being lost
a memory that blessed away their darkness.

Let us ride together, unexplainable
as small wind who touches & sings
without question. Listen. Listen:
No radiance is born from reason.
In this night of many heavens
even these words can be left behind.

Leanne Ponder *has made a living
interpreting dreams in a psychology lab,
painting carnival backdrops, writing poems
and fiction, teaching spies how to listen
effectively, pretending to be a barefoot
peddler, playing harp, and adapting
and performing traditional folktales,
among other occupations.*

*She now lives peacefully in Central Vermont,
with a loving husband, a feisty little dog,
and a big yellow cat.*

—June 2015

www.ingramcontent.com/pod-product-compliance
Lightning Source LLC
Chambersburg PA
CBHW031330040426
42443CB00005B/276